Within My Limits, I Pray

Talking to God About Illness, Disability and Life Changes

Joanne Ardolf Decker, Ph.D.

PublishAmerica
Baltimore

© 2009 by Joanne Ardolf Decker, Ph.D.
All rights reserved. No part of this book may be reproduced, stored in a retrieval system or transmitted in any form or by any means without the prior written permission of the publishers, except by a reviewer who may quote brief passages in a review to be printed in a newspaper, magazine or journal.

First printing

PublishAmerica has allowed this work to remain exactly as the author intended, verbatim, without editorial input.

Scripture taken from the HOLY BIBLE, NEW INTERNATIONAL VERSION. Copyright ©1973, 1978, 1984 International Bible Society. Used by permission of Zondervan Bible Publishers.

ISBN: 1-60836-643-X (softcover)
ISBN: 978-1-61582-357-4 (hardcover)
PUBLISHED BY PUBLISHAMERICA, LLLP
www.publishamerica.com
Baltimore

Printed in the United States of America

Dedication

This book is dedicated to all my care providers, past, present and future; in particular to my darling husband, Jim. His loving kindness is my lifeline.

Acknowledgments

I am indebted to Nicole Briar whose hands at the computer and her editing skills brought this to completion. My dear husband Jim was always there for support, scriptural references and proofreading. Many family members and friends encouraged me to complete this work: Barb Traxler, Fr. John Zuercher, SJ, Sister Rosemary Schwalbe, SSND, Sister Alene Kuhn, SSND and Sister Daniella Kuhn, SSND. Also, a big thank you to the good people at PublishAmerica, who managed the final stages. Of course, the Holy Spirit nudged me all along the way. Thank you!

Within My Limits, I Pray

*Talking to God About Illness,
Disability and Life Changes*

Introduction

My Story

It was the berries! That summer we had a wonderful crop of red raspberries. When my husband, Jim, and I picked them together, I couldn't sustain a reach to pick the best berries. Besides, he always had more in his bucket than I when we were finished. Something was wrong!

My family doctor referred me to a neurologist who gave me a painful test called electromyography, using electric shocks to test the responses of my muscles. Without hesitation he asked for a conference with Jim and me and pronounced my diagnosis: "You have a motor neuron disease, likely ALS (Amyotrophic Lateral

Sclerosis)—Lou Gehrig's disease. It is a degenerative and terminal disease. The nerves die, the muscles weaken and eventually you cannot breathe. You are likely to live 18 to 24 months. Go home and put your life together and do whatever you want." We were shocked and devastated. That was nearly 7 years ago—when Jim and I had been together for 28 years.

I met Jim when I taught in lower Brooklyn, New York. One weekend I went upstate to his hometown for a recreation conference that he attended. He was introduced to me by his coworker, and his first words to me were "Hey you're cute!" How could I resist that? After we danced a bit, he invited me out for a doughnut. Certainly no one could use that as a line! To make a long story short, we hit it off perfectly, were engaged in a month, and married two months later. If we were to do it all over again, we wouldn't wait so long!

We came back to my home state, Minnesota, for the wedding. I grew up on a farm where I was the youngest of five children. There were many skills to learn: cooking, baking, cleaning, raising flowers and vegetables, driving a tractor and caring for animals. I also enjoyed music, art, public speaking, and sports. In our life together, Jim and I enjoyed an active life while he worked in the field of recreation and I was a teacher.

I knew during the second week of first grade that I wanted to be a teacher, and I never changed my mind. Over the years I taught elementary school, high school, and many years in college back home in Minnesota. When I retired, I said, "I loved teaching, but now I love not teaching!" Jim and I traveled and continued our active lifestyle together. Who knew it would come to a screeching halt on a September day when a neurologist pronounced my diagnosis?

Following those devastating words, Jim and I cried, reminisced and prayed for the next three or four months. Finally, we knew crying was doing no good. We decided to just live one day at a time. We realized that, in many ways, we both had the disease. We were in it together.

We knew from the beginning that our faith would make all the difference. Without a belief in a loving God, the journey would be too difficult. I didn't believe this disease could come from God. The God I know is loving and wants only good for me. I knew I could rely on God, my dear husband, family and friends during the journey ahead.

Early on, I decided to make ALS my friend rather than an enemy. I knew many people who "battled" one disease or another; struggling against an enemy day by day. I did not want an enemy within me. I did not want hostility, anger and warfare in my life. If I made ALS a friend, we might get along and not "battle."

The years following the diagnosis have given me many emotions and issues to ponder. My way of grappling with them was to write and pray. I talked to God about things on my mind. The prayers in this book are compiled from my visits with God that came straight from my heart.

I believe hundreds and thousands of people struggle with the same thoughts and feelings I have. My intent is to share my prayers with others to help start their own visits with God. For some, these prayers could be read to them by someone else. Therefore, family members, care providers and volunteers might find this little book helpful as well.

I have already prayed these prayers not only for myself, but for my readers. I know that our compassionate God is with us at all times, ready to be our strength in weakness and our consolation in desolation.

Joanne Ardolf Decker, Ph.D.

Chapter I

Reality

Though petals fall, the plant still blooms.

What Is It?

After many tests, x-rays, blood draws and consultations the question still remains, "What is causing such havoc in my body?"

> *Now faith is the assurance of things hoped for, the conviction of things not seen. Hebrews 11:1*

Prayer

O God of Final Conclusions, you know my state of mind and my current madness while I anticipate a diagnosis. My heart hangs heavy with dull pain while I hang on, ponder and trust. I want to hope for the best, yet something tells me I must also plan for the worst.

O Beloved God, fill me with confidence, patience, serenity and peace. I believe you are with me, My Strength and My Hope. I ask you to prepare me for the answer to the question, "What is it?" no matter the outcome. I trust that your grace will be sufficient for me regardless the result. Open my heart to all your answers, now and always. Amen.

May I always accept the answers you have in store for me, My Caring God.

My own questions about my health to pray about…

Medical Tests

Tests are always on the agenda when medical professionals seek answers.

…but those who wait for the Lord shall renew their strength…
Isaiah 40:31a

Prayer

O God of All Answers, I ask you to provide answers through the multiple medical tests prescribed for my benefit these days. Let the results be clear and conclusive. Direct the technicians to perform their tasks efficiently, effectively, and with little discomfort to me, please! Make me brave, not grumpy during each procedure.

You are the one who understands my body better than anyone in this world, My Marvelous Maker. Through appropriate, approved tests, please reveal the irregularities that are causing difficulty for me so that proper treatments may follow. I place myself in your hands and in the hands of the professionals who understand the tests and how to read them. I trust in you, My God. Amen.

Show me and my health professionals what's wrong and what to do in the midst of my illness, My Healing God.

My own medical tests to pray about...

Blood Draws

The technician sticks the needle into my vein (when she can find it!) and out flows my blood, as though my very life is being drawn from the inside of me into the outside world.

For the life of the flesh is in the blood... Leviticus 17:11a

Prayer

O God of All Life and Love, when I see my blood flowing from my vein into a vial, I am in awe over the silent, complex functions at work in my body. The life blood that you gave me flows throughout my systems without my deliberation or awareness. Seeing my blood makes me contemplate the wonder of my life. My body is a magnificent miracle to be admired.

Thank you, O Source of All Life, for my life and for the very blood that flows through my veins. I also want to thank you for shedding your blood to save me. Let me accept the prick of a needle in gratitude for all that you endured for me. Amen.

By your blood I am saved, O Loving Savior. I am oh, so grateful!

My own experience with blood draws to pray about…

Diagnosis

Now I have the answer, but I don't want it!

It is the Lord who goes before you. He will be with you… do not fear or be dismayed. Deuteronomy 31:8

Prayer

O Venerable God, I feel more vulnerable than a newborn puppy. I have nauseating news that is too harsh to fathom. You let me enjoy good health for most of my life, and now I have a grave illness. How can this be? Could the doctors be wrong? Please let them be wrong!

O God of Gigantic Graces, you promised that your grace is always sufficient for us. I need that to be true. Grow my heart to lean on your grace, your strength, your courage, your boldness and bravery. Only with you at my side, holding my hand, can I go forward to live the journey that lies ahead. I trust in you. Amen.

Be with me on this journey, O Perfect Partner.

My own diagnoses to pray about…

Why?

Like a three-year old child I keep asking, "Why?" So many questions, so few answers.

I will keep watch to see what he will say to me, and what he will answer concerning my complaint. Habakkuk 2:1b

Prayer

O Answerable God, I come with questions that I know have no answers, but I seek them just the same. I wish you lived just down the block so I could run to your house and chat over a cup of coffee. I'd ask you a long list of questions and expect straightforward answers. I'm desperate to understand right now.

Your will is beyond my comprehension, My Wondrous God, so I don't expect to grasp why I have a wicked disease. I pray for strong faith as I strive to carry on, knowing that your love and support are always with me. I believe you want only good for me. I rely on you, I trust in you. Amen.

Your will has no why, O Gracious God.

My own questions to pray about…

Mourning

I believe mourning is some of life's hardest work, yet it is important to feel the feelings—all of them.

...mourning and crying and pain will be no more... Revelation 21:4b

Prayer

O God of Tears and Joy, I mourn the loss of the life I knew, and I anticipate more losses ahead. I grieve my wonderful life, yet I am grateful to be alive to look forward to more life adventures, whatever they may be. I cannot predict what lies ahead; only you know that, My All-knowing God. I trust you will never abandon me.

Take my tears, O Comforting Creator, and use them to sprinkle new life on my body and soul. Nurture me and those I love as we plod the journey ahead. When the passage is dark, light our way with your promises of joy. Amen.

I look to you for comfort and healing, My Consoling God.

My own feelings of loss to pray about...

Last-Time Syndrome

Seeing each event as a likely "last one" makes for a keener sense of what it is, increasing the urgency to make the most of it.

...hope in the Lord from this time on and forevermore. Psalm 131:3

Prayer

O Lasting Love, I come to you determined to let you choose the last time for people, places and things in my life. I tried to think about "last times," but I became depressed. I know now that I don't need to draw anything to a conclusion. That is your work, not mine.

My Everlasting God, reveal how I can enjoy the moments as they come along and not worry about how many more I may have. Your timing is perfect, and I trust that you will give me the perfect number of days filled with firsts and lasts and many in-betweens. I don't need to keep track. Amen.

My life is in your hands, O Loving Leader of my life.

My own "last time" experiences to pray about…

Denial

I can't tolerate constant awareness of my illness; denying it is a safety measure, a protection for my soul.

In this world you will have trouble, but take heart;
I have overcome the world. John 16:33

Prayer

O My Undeniable God, sometimes it feels downright good to deny my illness and just enjoy the moment. I know you are always with me, and I will never deny that. I believe you want me to live in the present and celebrate the gifts you send me every day. Guide me to relish life in spite of my illness. I trust that your loving presence will sustain me through all the circumstances I will ever face. For now, O Life-giving Lover, I want to participate fully in the joys and surprises of every day. Amen.

Though I may deny my illness, I will never deny you, My Undeniable God.

My own episodes of denial to pray about…

Depression

My illness leaves me "down in the dumps" from time to time, and although that may be normal, I don't like it.

> *Why are you cast down, O my soul, and why are you disquieted within me? Psalm 42: 5a*

Prayer

O Vital Spirit, I am told that depression is one stage of loss, so I can expect it to hang around my illness and its many losses. I notice, though, that depression can be contagious, and I don't want to affect others with my melancholy.

Come into my life and surround me with your vigor, verve and vitality. I don't want to feel sorry for myself. Instead, I want to overcome my depression by depending on you and deepening my relationship with you. Your love is enough reason for joy.

Make clear how to focus on goodness and the bountiful gifts you give me. I hope to make known to others the bounty of your blessings. Let me positively influence others rather than bring them down with negativity. I choose my love for you to be contagious. Amen.

Lift my spirits with your love, O Gentle, Loving Spirit.

My own feelings of sadness to pray about…

Fear

Shutting down my fear-spinning mind is a never-ending contest. On the other hand, living in fear only breeds more harm.

I sought the Lord, and he answered me, and delivered me from all my fears. Psalm 34:4

Prayer

O Fearless God, I know you understand my fearful moments, and I beg for fewer of them. I believe it is one thing to be afraid from time to time; another to have a spirit of fear within me. Instead I yearn for a spirit of hope, faith, trust and love.

Draw me deep into your heart, My God of Pure Love, to trust in you and the plans you have for me. With you in my heart, all my fears will be transformed into confidence, joy and love. Dash my doubts against a stone just as you foil other enemies who seek to take me down. Amen.

I trust in you, O God of Courage.

My own fearful thoughts to pray about…

Dreams

Perhaps in my dreams I am striving to accept the realities of my life with illness.

...and he dreamed that there was a ladder...and the angels of God were ascending and descending on it. Genesis 28:12

Prayer

O God of My Dreams, like people throughout history, I try to understand my dreams, but it seems impossible to know their real meaning. Lately, I find myself dreaming about living with my weaknesses and disabilities. Perhaps my dreams are your way of showing me my new self, helping me adjust to my new truth. Give me courage as I face myself in these dreams, My Gracious Friend, but not be overly concerned about them. I place myself in your hands whether I am awake or asleep. Spending my eternity with you is the only dream I need to come true. Amen.

When I dream I want to dream about you, My Understanding God.

My own to dreams to ponder and pray about...

Doctors

Oh how I need doctors who serve me in meaningful ways!

Thus you will know them by their fruits. Matthew 7:20

Prayer

O Master of Medicine, please bless me with doctors who have excellent skills, knowledge, competence and inspiring values. Let them respect me and understand me. I seek doctors who know you, My Healing God. I wish for doctors who will lean on you while they seek answers and treatments to extend your healing touch to me. Give them ample rest, open hearts, attentive listening, wisdom, good judgment, loving words, skillful hands, and virtuous spirits. Please prompt me to let them know when I appreciate them. Amen.

Please guide all doctors to find the answers they seek, O Perfect Healer.

My own concerns regarding doctors to pray about…

Good and Bad Days

I do not understand what causes good and bad days, but I do know that days are not equal when it comes to how I feel.

Satisfy us in the morning with your steadfast love, so that we may rejoice and be glad all our days. Psalm 90:14

Prayer

O God of My Days and Nights, thank you for the good days and I ask you to limit the bad ones. When I feel well I consider the day a blessing, but when my illness takes control the day is not what the doctor ordered.

Oh, don't get me wrong, My Gracious God, I appreciate the gift of every day, including those that bring more difficulties than others. However, when I feel energized my spirits soar and my smile comes without prompting. I want always to praise and glorify you with a joyful spirit, O Praiseworthy God, so I ask you to grant me peace and quiet joy every day regardless of how I feel. Amen.

Thank you for every day, My Life-giving God.

My own good and bad days to pray about…

Aches and Pains

Amazing how discomfort tires me out and makes it hard to focus on anything but myself. There is a certain loneliness in this distress.

Rejoice in hope, be patient in suffering, persevere in prayer.
Romans 12:12

Prayer

O My God of Comfort and Consolation, I come today with aches and pains, and I admit to feeling sorry for myself. Please pardon my self-centeredness. I want to concentrate on you and your many gifts rather than wallow in self-pity. Let me remember all the pain-free days you gave me throughout my life. Direct me to endure this aggravation.

You understand my body and how it feels, O Compassionate Companion. I know that I am not alone in my discomfort. I offer my soreness in gratitude for all that you suffered for me. Please give me resilience to make it through this day and look forward to another day when my body will be less troublesome. Amen.

I offer you these aches and pains, My Redeeming God, as reminders of all you did for me through your redemptive love.

My own aches and pains to pray about…

Slow Motion

My life is a slow motion movie with every move deliberate and premeditated.

But if we hope for what we do not see, we wait for it with patience. Romans 8:25

Prayer

O Mighty, Moving God, I move very slowly these days because of my illness, and I feel frustrated in both body and mind. I come to you asking for patience with myself. I would like to scamper about as I did most of my life, but now you are asking me to slow down and be comfortable in this sluggish state. Teach me to appreciate my every move and be grateful for each slow but sure step.

Remind me, O God of Perfect Timing, that your ways are seldom swift or hurried. Teach me to be tolerant just as you are patient with me and all humans. You don't push us but rather lead us toward you, inch by inch. Teach me your ways. Amen.

Slowly, surely, safely, I want to make my way to you, My Timeless God.

My own frustrations to pray about…

Falling

Falling is the ultimate embarrassment of human beings. We are meant to be upright, not on our backs or butts or hands and knees.

On their hands they will bear you up, so that you will not dash your foot against a stone. Psalm 91:12

Prayer

O Upright God, I come to you with poor balance and a tendency to fall. I despise finding myself on the ground, humiliated, self-conscious, and in a state of disgrace. I am grateful to have avoided injuries so far. Good padding helps!

What is it that I should learn from falling? Is it a keener recognition of my humanity? Is it a warning to be more careful? No, this lesson is best: when I fall I know how much I need you, My Loving Savior. Please keep me balanced, body and soul, sure-footed on my journey toward you. Amen.

O God of Good Balance, keep me from falling. Keep me upright in every way.

My own falls to pray about…

Struggles

This illness has brought new struggles into my life; I want to keep trying rather than give up.

Cast your burden on the Lord and he will sustain you. Psalm 55:22a

Prayer

O God of Comfort and Ease, bless me with power to manage the physical, emotional and spiritual struggles that come with every day. I want to carry on a normal life as long as I am able. I know that only you can empower me to do that.

When my limbs rebel, O Merciful Maker, redirect my needs, distract me from pain, and divert my attention from me to you. Remind me of my own rebellious ways, and how much you love me. Let me appreciate this body in spite of its quirks and struggles. Guide me to be grateful for what I still can do. Amen.

I cast all my struggles on you, My Powerful and Comforting God.

My own struggles to pray about…

Turning over in Bed

A frightening aspect of my illness is not having command of my body.

…I meditate on you in the watches of the night; for you have been my help… Psalm 63:6b-7a

Prayer

O God of Tender Turns, my body is growing more and more uncooperative, and I'm often annoyed when I can't accomplish something as simple as rolling over in bed.

I feel my body is insolent, insulting me, attacking my very life.

Help me, My Patient Partner, to be calm, enduring and gentle in the midst of my frustrations. I ask for a tranquil, composed and unruffled spirit when I wrestle with physical movements. I don't want to get exasperated and exhausted. Rather, I count on your strength and envision you rolling me into your arms where you will strengthen me. Secure me and steep me in your love. Amen.

Turn me into your loving arms, O God of All My Strength.

My own turns to pray about…

Weakness

Weakness is part of my illness now, but I don't want it to be part of my character.

> *…but he said to me, "My grace is sufficient for you, for power is made perfect in weakness." 2 Corinthians 12:9*

Prayer

O Powerful God, I come to you in my weakness to depend on your energy and strength. When my body is too weak to lift, carry or move, provide me patience and strength of character to make the necessary adjustments and refrain from anger and frustration.

Having weakness in my body is one thing, O Mighty God, but I don't want to have a weak spirit. I pray that my physical weakness may strengthen my inner self. Give me a strong, durable soul fixed on you. Purify me in my weakness. I believe your grace is sufficient for me. Amen.

I am weak but you are strong, O God of All Power and Might.
I depend on you and trust you. I believe you will always support me.

My own weakness to pray about…

Fatigue

Worn out; washed up; spun dry; shot; not so hot; best forgot. This body feels used up right now, and I'm tired of being tired.

...but those who wait for the Lord shall renew their strength; they shall mount up with wings like eagles, they shall walk and not faint. Isaiah 40:29

Prayer

O My Untiring God, you know my weariness even when I deny it. Perhaps you allow me to grow tired so I will surrender and come to you for recovery. Help me to realize the positive side of fatigue—the wonder of rejuvenation. When I am tired I want to bask in your gentle, reviving energy where I can rest and absorb your goodness. Let me relax in your arms, O Serene Supremacy, where I am safe and free from exhaustion. Renew my spirit with wings like eagles. With you at my side, I shall not faint but be refreshed. Amen.

I wait for you, My God, to replace my fatigue with energy, vigor and joy.

My own fatigue to pray about...

My Appearance

I'd prefer a layer of make up to disguise me, but that still wouldn't change the truth. Perhaps the real transformation I need is in my heart.

And all of us, with unveiled faces, seeing the glory of the Lord as though reflected in a mirror, are being transformed into the same image from one degree of glory to another... 2 Corinthians 3:18.

Prayer

O My Beautiful God, just one glance in the mirror is enough to confirm that I resemble a bowl of mushroom-soup today. This color is genuine evidence of illness, and I would rather not face that reality.

I know your love for me does not depend on the color of my cheeks. Whether my skin looks ashen or bright, murky or clear, I am sure you love me and care for me. Let me be more concerned about the character of my soul in your sight than about the appearance of my body.

O All Reflecting God, let my mirror image today lead me to see you face to face. Please prepare me by transforming me into glory from one degree to another. I want to look more like you every day. Give me hope in the makeover that will one day clothe me in the full color of your glory. Amen.

O Radiant, Loving God, all I want is to be beautiful in your sight.

My own concerns about appearance to pray about…

Reaching

It's a maddening feeling to see what I want, know exactly how to get it, yet be unable to accomplish such a simple task.

God is our refuge and strength, a very present help in trouble. Psalm 46:1

Prayer

O Far-reaching God, I must have made a million successful reaches in my life; I never appreciated one of them until now when reaching is troublesome. I have taken most of my actions for granted, and I'm sorry for that. Now I want to appreciate even small movements. Give me tolerance of my body and let me reach a state of peace rather than frustration.

When my physical reaching is disappointing, O Triumphant Trinity, turn my thoughts to you. Remind me that reaching for you is what counts. Stretch my heart and my soul sufficiently to attain your graces. Convert my physical aggravation into far-reaching growth for my soul. Amen.

Teach me how to reach for your love, My Sustaining God.

My own struggles with reaching to pray about…

Muscle Cramps

When muscles cramp, they hurt; it's difficult to quiet them.

…he will renew you in his love… Zephaniah 3:17c

Prayer

When my muscles pull and twist and cramp, O Straightforward God, all I do is tighten up and shriek. I am sorry to be such a coward. These cramping muscles are a quandary to me. Help me, My Wise Teacher, to know what to learn from them.

Perhaps my cramping muscles are a reminder of my stubborn ways that pulled me from you too often. In my turning away I always made things worse and found myself in pointless spiritual pain. Thank you, O Relentless God, for pursuing me, quieting me, and tugging me toward you even when I rebelled. I know for certain that you are a persistent God who loves me. Amen.

Quiet my body and soul with your love, O Loving God.

My own muscle pain to pray about…

Regrets

Although regrets are useless, they can be a menace for my mind.

For godly grief produces a repentance that leads to salvation and brings no regret…2 Corinthians 7:10

Prayer

O Ever Present God, being able to look back on my life seems to be both a blessing and a bother. The blessing is reminiscing. I love to think back on pleasant times, good people, beautiful places and things that filled my life. However, here and there come twists and turns that form regrets. I wish I could leave them alone. I cannot change a thing from my past, but an unfulfilled wish or hope or dream can plague me from time to time.

Only in you, My Perfect Partner, do I find solace and acceptance of my life, just as I lived it. Clear my heart of regrets, and let me appreciate every piece of my life. I bring my life to you, confident of your love, grace and mercy. Amen.

Into your hands I place my life, my all accepting God.

My own regrets or lack of regrets to pray about…

Chapter II

Adjustments

Though roads have curves, make matching turns.

Attitude Adjustment

I could make my life easier if I kept a better attitude.

Trust in the Lord with all your heart, and do not rely on your own insight. Proverbs 3:5

Prayer

O God of My Life, I realize I need an attitude adjustment if I am to manage my life changes. Feeling sorry for myself, with a "poor me" mentality, is not working very well. My weakness pulls my spirits down. I want to draw myself up and be strong. I need your help.

Only in you, My God of Pure Power, can I hope to sift out negatives and see positives in my life. Strengthen me in every positive way. Like a humming bird, I want to see what is sweet rather than be a vulture seeking decay. I want to be a breath of fresh air, not a cold draft for myself or others. Breathe into me a new spirit. Amen.

I want to positively live with you, My Perfect Creator.

My own attitudes to pray about…

My Diet

Because of my illness, I have certain things I can and cannot eat.

"I have food to eat that you do not know about." John 4:31

Prayer

O All-providing God, thank you for my taste buds and for the foods that I can eat. Let me be grateful for each morsel that I consume and give me the good sense to stick to the diet that is best for my body. I want to appreciate the foods I can eat rather than grieve over those I can't have.

When I consider the needs of people around the world, I know that hundreds of thousands are hungry every day while my nutritional needs are met. O Generous God, I value the bounty you provide me and my family. I pray for all people of the world to have sufficient food for good nutrition, and let them enjoy some fun foods just as I do. Amen.

Thank you, My Great Giving God, for food and good nutrition.

My own dietary needs to pray about…

Financial Affairs

Illness is one thing we try to insure ourselves against, but when faced head on, the paperwork abounds and red tape proliferates.

Trust in the Lord with all your heart, and do not rely on your own insight. Proverbs 3:5

Prayer

My All Assuring God, I have never been good at reading the exacting language and fine print of insurance policies. I have been able to leave that to others more skilled in such matters, but not everyone has that luxury. Please grant my family and me ongoing good judgment regarding future financial affairs.

You are the ultimate protection I need, O Glorious Guardian. Keep me aware that my destination lies with you, and things like financial affairs affect only temporary circumstances. Matters of this world are often too complex for my limited mind to grasp, but I trust that you will always insure my welfare and make me the beneficiary of your love. That's all the protection I will ever need. Amen.

Protect me from all evil, My Perfect Protector.

My own financial matters to pray about…

How Are You?

It is an often-heard question in our society, "How are you?" Now that I'm ill, it's harder than ever to answer that question.

*May the God of hope fill you with all joy and peace in believing,
so that you may abound in hope by the power of the Holy Spirit.*
Romans 15:13

Prayer

O God of Constant Concern, I believe that your love is steady and steeped in concern for me. You are with me always, and you know the answer to the question, "How are you?" I don't even need to use words; you know. Thank you for your devoted care for me.

When I hear that question, My Amazing Answering God, teach me to be honest yet gentle in what I say and how I share. I want to draw others into deeper friendship rather than bore them with details about my condition. Instead, let me share your work in my life so that others, too, may be aware of you. Amen.

With you at my side, O Loving Creator, I will always be just fine.

My own answers to "How are you?" to pray about…

Beyond "Looking Good"

Looks can be deceiving. People often tell me I "look good," but what they see isn't the reality I feel.

> *...for the Lord does not see as mortals see; they look on the outward appearance, but the Lord looks on the heart.*
> *1 Samuel 16:7b*

Prayer

O My Good-looking God, thank you for all the days when people think I look good in spite of my illness. You and I both know that there are plenty other days when I don't look so great, so let's make the most of the good ones, right? I don't want to be sarcastic or cynical when people tell me I look good, yet feel otherwise. Give me words that express gratitude, but keep me from being superficial or shallow.

More than physically looking good I want my soul to be good-looking in your sight. I yearn to measure up to your plans for me and your expectations of my spiritual growth. I want to grow in deeper love with you. Amen.

I always want to look good in your sight, My Beautiful God.

My own true self to pray about…

Pats on the Shoulder

I notice that sometimes people give me a certain pat on the shoulder when they approach me. I don't know if it means, "Oh, you poor thing!" or "I'm praying for you" or "I'm here for you" or "I know how you feel."

And in their prayers for you, their hearts will go out to you, because of the surpassing grace God has given you. 2 Corinthians 9:14

Prayer

O Speaker of All Languages, help me to understand the touch of others that I often feel on my shoulder. I don't want to read it as a "pity pat" that makes me feel less than whole. Although I'm ill, I am still the person I always was. Instead, I want to understand it as kindness from one heart to another, from their spirit to mine. I realize that other people want to extend their love to me, and their touch is one way to convey care and affection. O Great Healer of My Life, let me be open to your surpassing grace as it comes to me through others. Amen.

O *Loving Lord, let me feel your caring touch.*

My own "pats on the shoulder" to pray about…

Compassion

Nothing brings the reality of illness to light like being ill myself. My illness has given me new eyes for others and their circumstances.

…who redeems your life from the Pit, who crowns you with steadfast love and mercy; Psalm 103:4

Prayer

O Compassionate Companion, why is it so difficult to relate to others in their infirmity, grief or dejection? Since we are all human it should be easy to feel what others feel, to experience the pains, emotions, or troubles of another; but it is not so. We humans strive to feel with others knowing that our compassion will always be limited. Teach me how to relate to the needs of others. Most Understanding God, I want to be of service to others if possible and show them the kind of consideration you show me.

I know that you feel with me far more than anyone else can, and that brings me great comfort. You dwell within me, live with me, are so close to me that you know how I feel even before I am aware. Thank you for your complete kindness. You are the perfect model of empathy. Show me your ways. Amen.

Teach me to feel with others, O Loving God of Compassion.

My own compassion to pray about…

Shopping

Without wheels on scooters and wheelchairs, shopping would be a thing of the past for me.

With the Lord at my side I do not fear.
What can mortals do to me? Psalm 118:6

Prayer

Shopping has become a tricky operation, O Master of Markets. My limitations present complications to my shopping sprees. I need ease and comfort to get the job done. Guide me to short distances, uncrowded spaces, shelves I can reach and suitable sales. You know how I love a bargain! Teach me to be patient in the stores, My Cordial God. I want to be considerate and grateful to still be able to shop. Amen.

Take me to the markets that meet my needs, O Helpful God.

My own shopping needs to pray about...

One Day at a Time

Living with illness now, I seem to manage best if I focus on just one day at a time.

This is the day the Lord has made, let us rejoice and be glad in it. Psalm 118:24

Prayer

O Ever Present God, living in the present is not easy for us mortals. We like to know what's ahead of us, but you are the only one who knows what's in store. We cannot change the past, but we can get stuck in memories. I come to you trusting that your love will sustain me both now and always.

Dear God of All My Days, I want to take one day at a time rejoicing and living each moment to the utmost. Show me how to patiently approach each day's challenges and look to you for the answers to problems and concerns as they come up. I place my trust in you, My God. I want to think as James Dean would say "Dream as if you'll live forever, live as if you'll die today." Amen.

Thank you, My God, for every day…one at a time!

My own present, past, and future to pray about…

Being Prayed For

What a humbling experience it is to be prayed for.

The prayer of the righteous is powerful and effective. James 5:16b

Prayer

O Extraordinary God, I feel very ordinary, and yet I am blessed with extraordinary family and friends who continue to plead my cause before you, sending prayers from their hearts to yours on my behalf. Thank you for the people you place in my life, who seek to help me through prayer.

I come to you, O Listening Lover, praying for all those who pray for me. I ask you to bless them with answers to their prayers for their own lives just as they extend their prayers for me. You know all that is in their hearts. Grant them their hearts desires. Amen.

O Generous God, I pray that you bless those who pray for me.

My own prayer connections to pray about…

Let the Phone Ring

Answering the phone after one or two rings used to be a typical pattern for me; no more.

"Speak, Lord, for your servant is listening." 1 Samuel 3:10b

Prayer

O God of All Connections, please bless those who call me by phone and nudge them to let the rings continue a bit longer these days. My world is limited right now, as you know My God, and the telephone is a key connection to the wider world; I don't want to discourage others from trying to reach me.

I am enormously grateful that you give me ample time to respond to your calls, O Ever-calling God. I know that you try to reach me often though I am frequently slow to respond, just as I am slow to answer my ringing phone. Let me never discount your calls or the calls of others. Amen.

Thank you for my connections to others, My Loving God.

My own communications to pray about…

Giving Up Control

To willingly give up control is a trial for me.

Let your hand be ready to help me for I have chosen your precepts.
Psalm 119:173

Prayer

O God of All Authority, take me by the hand and lead me as you wish. You place others in my life to be in charge of matters that I no longer can manage. Thank you for them, and I beg to be open to their ways. Let me allow them to take your place as my leader and director.

O Mighty Manager, I open my hands and my heart to you asking you to take control over my life and show me how to yield to your loving ways. I find it difficult to say, "yes" to you, but I yearn for a willing, accepting, and compliant heart. Amen.

You perfectly control my life, O Loving Leader.

My own control issues to pray about…

Care Giving and Receiving

Giving and receiving go together like the two sides of a coin. These days I am on the receiving side; it is not easy.

> *…and whoever gives even a cup of water to one of these little ones in the name of a disciple, truly I tell you, none of these will lose their reward. Matthew 10:42*

Prayer

O Most Gracious Giver, although you are the ultimate caregiver in my life, you place in my midst many other generous people to serve my needs. They are willing to help me, and I thank you for all of them. Now my work is to receive their gifts of loving care.

Teach me to be grateful, amenable to new ways, and agreeable to procedures that originate from my caregivers. I want to be a boon not a burden, a joy not a problem, a blessing not a liability, a delight not a drain. I want to be like you, My Amiable God. Amen.

Thank you for my caregivers, My Ever-caring God.

My own care givers to pray about…

My Cane

My cane is light, strong and supports my every move.

Even though I walk through the darkest valley, I fear no evil, for you are with me; your rod and your staff—they comfort me.
Psalm 23:4

Prayer

O My Supportive God, let me lean on you the way I lean on my cane for security and stability. Please prevent me from falling in every way, body and soul. Let my cane be a reminder of the steadiness you give me in my life.

Thank you for the willow tree that gave part of its life to be my cane, O Maker of Magnificence. The beauty that grew into the wood enhances its function. May I always be grateful for the support I get from my cane and from you, My Devoted God. Amen.

Let me always lean on you, O God, My True Support.

My own support to pray about…

My Walker

My walker has four wheels to roll with me as I walk, and it has a nifty seat for me to plunk onto when walking or standing gets tiresome. My walker virtually sustains my lifestyle.

…Jesus himself came near and walked with them, but their eyes were kept from recognizing him. Luke 24:15

Prayer

My Beloved God, as I lean on my walker to make my way from one place to another I ask you to walk with me. Be my prop for support and my respite when I need to rest. You are always with me, and I rely on you, O Reliable God.

My walker is a vivid reminder of my need for support. I am weak in both body and soul. Without you, My God of Strength and Mercy, I am nothing. You give me reason to walk onward even when pain or depression takes me down. I believe in you, I hope in you, I love you. I trust in your love. Amen.

Walk with me through thick and thin, My Unfailing God.

My own lifestyle to pray about…

My Wheelchair

A marvelous invention—four wheels on a chair to help me move about.

WITHIN MY LIMITS, I PRAY

*For surely I know the plans I have for you, says the Lord;
plans for your welfare and not for harm... Jeremiah 29:11a*

Prayer

My All Providing God, thank you for the wheelchairs you have made available for me and for others. It is quite an adventure to be pushed in the wheelchair by someone else. I become that person's body, moving at his or her speed, depending on his or her skills, eyes, strength, perception and judgment. I am learning to surrender and just enjoy the ride. Thank you for those who look after my needs by supplying strength and movement to get me from one place to another.

You are in charge of everything including my life, O Maneuvering Master. However, too often I find it difficult to let go and let you take me where you wish, where your plans are best for me. I want to give you full control of my life the way I yield control to one who pushes my wheelchair. Please maneuver as you wish. I'll sit tight and enjoy the ride! Amen.

I place myself in your hands, O Loving Leader of My Life.

My own journeys to pray about...

Eating Out

Eating out used to be easier than eating at home but now the reverse is true.

*He brought me to the banqueting house, and his intention toward
me was love. Song of Solomon 2:4*

Prayer

O Source of All Sustenance, please be near to ease the experience when I go out to eat. Help me to make the best of every situation, and help others feel secure in their eagerness to lend a hand. I want to maximize the moments when family and friends gather to dine out, but please diminish my discomfort in those situations. Dine with us, comfort us, and show us your tender goodness.

When you were on earth, Dear Jesus, you ate with your friends often, both before and after your resurrection. I look forward to dining with you, My Beloved Friend. Please grant me a place at your eternal banquet, which I know will be barrier free. Amen.

Be my dining guest, My God of All Goodness.

My own dining to pray about...

Asking for Help

Why is it distasteful to ask for help? For most of my adult life I found it easy to help others and delighted when someone asked for my assistance. Now I am often in need, yet I hesitate to ask.

For you have been my help, and in the shadow of your wings
I sing for joy.
Psalm 63:7

Prayer

O Heavenly Helper, I come asking for help from you when I need assistance from others. Sometimes I find it difficult to admit that I am unable to manage matters on my own. Fade my pride to accept a helping hand. Lead me to be gracious and grateful for assistance.

You are my might, O Powerful One. Every day brings occasions that point out my need for help. Please quiet my need to lead and teach me cordial surrender to others and loving surrender to you. Amen.

O Gracious God, thank you for the helpers you give me, and teach me to graciously accept the generous service of others.

My own need for help to pray about…

Miracles

I believe in miracles, big ones and small ones.

You are the God who works wonders… Psalm 77:14a

Prayer

O Master of Miracles, right now I would appreciate a huge miracle that would cure me instantly so I could resume the life I knew. I wish you were touchable so I could rush to meet you, tell you my needs, and have you reach out and cure me.

Although you are not in the flesh, I experience your spirit and your miracles. You provide people who cheer me, beauty to quiet my spirit and joy to heal my soul. You orchestrate "coincidence" and dissolve the impossible. Thank you for your work in my life.

Prepare me to receive your phenomenal wonders as I anticipate your daily miracles. Amen.

Work your wonders in my life, O Maker of Miracles.

My own miracles to pray about…

Acceptance

I've made up my mind to embrace my illness, learn what I must from it, and make the most of my life with or without it.

A tranquil mind gives life to the flesh… Proverbs 14:30a

Prayer

O All Accepting God, you allowed an illness along my life path. I come to you accepting that reality, yet I ask that you heal me if possible. I choose to embrace this condition hoping to learn from it and become a better person, a stronger soul. Please be gentle as you teach me life lessons. I am weak and sometimes frightened; nevertheless I place myself in your hands. I trust you, My Loving Friend, to hold my hand and sustain me along this journey. Amen.

I say "yes" to you, My Accepting God.

My own level of acceptance to pray about…

My Legal Will

"Put your affairs in order" is a suggestion that often accompanies the diagnosis of illness, especially a terminal illness.

*Into your hand I commit my spirit; you have redeemed me,
O Lord, faithful God. Psalm 31:5*

Prayer

My Orderly God, I come to you more aware than ever that I will not live forever, and I want to set my affairs in order, especially the affairs of my soul. Although I want to save my family from red tape in matters of finance and property, those things seem easy to handle compared to being secure in my spiritual estate.

My spiritual doubts and fears are ever in motion, but I yearn for a peace-filled heart prepared for life with you, O God of My Will. Take my doubts and fears and transform them into love for the new life that you promised. I trust you will never change your mind but rather keep your promises and let me be the beneficiary of your eternal gifts. Amen.

My will is to do your will, My Loving God.

My own material and spiritual wealth to pray about…

My Living Will

"Living Will" seems to be a silly title for something that addresses basic aspects of dying. It helps, nonetheless, in facing critical questions that must be confronted.

For to me, living is Christ and to die is gain. Philippians 1:21

Prayer

My Eternal God, I believe I was made to live in heaven. This world is not my permanent home. I am simply on my journey to your house where I hope to live with you forever. As much as I love my life here, I believe the home you are preparing for me will far surpass this temporary state.

Although I would like to have length of days here on earth I do not seek to extend my time here any longer than you wish, O Perfect Planner of My Life. I surrender to your will, your plans, and your designs for me. My living will is to accept your will. Amen.

I want to know and do your will, My Loving God.

My own living will to pray about…

Living with Illness

When it comes time for my last day I want to be remembered as someone who truly lived, not someone who just waited to die.

Instead you ought to say, "If the Lord wishes, we will live and do this or that." James 4:15

Prayer

O Living God, thank you for my precious life to enjoy for many years. Now that I live with illness I want more than ever to relish each day's unique joys and blessings. Even aches, pains and obstacles are useful because they let me know that I'm still alive.

Teach me, My Precious God, to be fully alive and to make the most of the moments you give me. Prepare me to carry on through thick and thin, during good days and bad, with you in mind, Dear Jesus. You are my model for living. Teach me your ways. Amen.

I want to live each day to the fullest, My Living God.

My own health to pray about…

Aging

Aging—what a complex phenomenon it is!

Satisfy us in the morning with your steadfast love, so that we may rejoice and be glad all our days. Psalm 90:14

Prayer

O God of All Ages, life seems to be filled with one thing after another, and on top of all that come complications of aging. How can I tell whether the things I feel are natural or un-natural? Since my own aging is new to me, I am not sure what to expect; what exactly is happening to me? I am depending on you to help me make sense of this experience.

My later years have crept up little by little, My Ageless God. I hardly noticed until I found myself walking slower, getting tired early in the day, and finding wrinkles and gray hair in the mirror. Isn't it strange—we all want to live a long time yet the idea of growing old is not a favorite. I want to make the most of the life you gave me, My Generous God. Open my heart and my mind to accept the self that I am becoming as days and years go by. More than anything, I want my aging soul to become beautiful in your site. Amen.

I want to age into a beautiful person, O Most Beautiful God.

My own aging to pray about…

Chapter III

Routines

Though days seem same, each one's a gift.

Routine

I know what to expect and find pleasure in the prospects that come with routine.

*And after you have suffered for a little while, the God of all grace…
will himself restore, support, strengthen, and establish you. I Peter 5:10*

Prayer

Please be with me on a routine basis, My Steady, Stable God. A certain amount of routine is necessary in my life these days because other people are involved in my care, and some things must be done in certain ways at certain times. However, it is you who bestows security, granting me ongoing assurance and never changing promises.

O Most Certain God, clear my heart of fears, judgments, worries and uncertainties. Replace them with routine peace, serenity, harmony and assurance of your love. Amen.

Keep me close to you on a routine basis, My Unchanging God.

My own routines to pray about…

Medications

Medications are an amazing phenomenon of our generation. When I down them, how do they know where to go and what to do?

*…there will grow all kinds of trees.… Their fruit will be for
food and their leaves for healing. Ezekiel 47: 12a;c*

Prayer

O Mighty Medicine Maker, I bring you my medications and ask you to bless them as they enter my body on their way to perform healing functions. Please let them hasten my healing.

Although medications are a creative attempt to mend irregularities in my body it is you, O Ultimate Healer, who holds authority over my health. I place my trust in you. You are my supreme medicine, my unsurpassed remedy, and I ask you to restore my health to me. Your will be done. Amen.

May my medications benefit my body this very day, My Loving God.

My own medications to pray about…

Alternative Treatments

Vitamins, herbs, acupuncture, and food supplements all seem to make a positive difference for me.

Trust in the Lord with all your heart, and do not rely on your own insight. Proverbs 3:5

Prayer

O God of Endless Alternatives, our world has a wide variety of treatments for abnormalities. Thank you for the traditional and nontraditional treatments which are available to me. I pray to choose sensible alternatives and not act out of desperation, but out of wisdom.

I give my health, my healing and my wellness to you, O

Heavenly Healer. Be my leader along the journey of my illness and guide my decisions so that I choose what fits my total health. I want to be as well as possible, physically, mentally, emotionally and spiritually. Show me how to proceed. Let me remember that you are My Ultimate Healer. I lay my life in your hands. Amen.

Show me the ways that are best for me, My Loving, Healing God.

My own considerations of alternative treatments to pray about…

Vitamins

Gathered from their containers, they are a little community ready to fight oxidation, build immunity, defy diseases and even help each other to be functional.

Now faith is the assurance of things hoped for, the conviction of things unseen. Hebrews 11:1

Prayer

O Trustworthy God, every day I take vitamins trusting they will benefit my health. In spite of their mysterious work, I believe they help me, and I surrender to take them time after time.

Vitamins lead me to contemplate my faith in you, My Impressive God, and your remarkable work in my life. Without my attention, with faultless timing and relentless nudging, you are ever at work to share your love with me. I believe in you, I hope in you, I trust you. Please steer my spirit straight ahead and spread health to my body and my soul every day. Amen.

O God of Good Health, improve my physical and spiritual health, I pray.

My own bodily mysteries to pray about…

Acupuncture

For thousands of years people in eastern cultures have found healing through a treatment known as acupuncture. For me the results are observable and definite.

Bless the Lord…who forgives all your iniquity, who heals all your diseases… Psalm 103:2-3

Prayer

O Benevolent God, thank you for the benefits I receive from acupuncture. I appreciate this age-old treatment that is proving to be useful to me just as it has been to people over the centuries. You are an amazing healer, and your ways are diverse and often mysterious. I don't need to know how your methods work; I am more than pleased with good results.

When I feel the acupuncture needles being inserted into my body, O Penetrating God, I want to think of you and ask you to penetrate every fiber of my being with your love and healing. Make your way through the thick skin of my being and fill me with goodness, kindness, uprightness and virtue. Amen.

Pierce me with your love and healing, O Great Healer of My Life.

My own health methods to pray about…

Back Rubs

With every back rub I feel the gift of loving touch, and it is oh so health-giving!

> *In your presence there is fullness of joy; in your right hand are pleasures forevermore. Psalm 16:11*

Prayer

Come, O Healing Hand of God, rub my body and my soul with your deep love until I am pliable, loving and compassionate. I want to relax in your arms and become gentle of heart, supple in spirit and free from anxiety in body and mind.

Thank you for the human hands that give me back rubs. I relish their restorative touch. Extend your life-giving healing through them. May my caregivers' hands remind me of your ever-present care for me and keep me aware of your willingness to make me whole. Since I must wait for your wholeness, help me endure limitations until that time. Meanwhile I'll enjoy my back rubs! Amen.

Massage both my body and my soul with your love, O Healing God.

My own healing touch to pray about…

E-mail

Checking e-mail is common to my day, like going to the mailbox used to be. I can do it with ease and never encounter bad weather.

> *"…it is the Lord your God who goes with you; he will not fail you or forsake you." Deuteronomy 31:6b*

Prayer

O Great Communicator, thank you for the connections I have with others in the world through electronic mail. The talents of others brought this invention to life, and I enjoy its fruits. It is convenient, quick and easy. I think you, too, might have enjoyed using it when you were on earth.

I am grateful to correspond with you in easier ways, My Ever-present God. Since you are always with me, I can speak my heart to you anytime. I don't have to remember your e-mail address or check my spelling before sending the message. With you, My Eternal Connection, e-mail stands for endless mail—conversations that are eternal. Amen.

Stay in touch with me, O Loving God.

My electronic communications to pray about…

Praying

It is not easy to pray during illness.

> *…for we do not know how to pray as we ought, but that very Spirit intercedes with sighs too deep for words. Romans 8:26*

Prayer

O God of My Prayers, I know that you are always with me whether I'm praying or not feeling up to it. Being ill makes it even more difficult. I want to have a rich prayer life; however I fall far from that goal. Teach me how to pray, O Holy Spirit. Dwell deep within me and know my prayers before I can even say them. Give me thoughts, words and actions that praise, glorify, and thank you. I ask your forgiveness and petition for needs according to your will. Amen.

Teach me how to pray, My Ever-listening God.

My own praying to pray about…

Exercising

Sit up, bend forward, a bit further, and a little further, and still more; and again and again. Kick heels high, stretch those shins, wiggle the ankles, knees under chin…and so the exercises go.

…with a strong hand and an outstretched arm, his steadfast love endures forever. Psalm 136:12

Prayer

O Lively, Loving God, although my exercise routine has become quite restricted I am grateful for the stretches I still can manage. I strive to stretch my soul, along with my body, that my spirit grows pliable, flexible and supple.

You are the foundation of my life, O Source of Strength and

Power. I want to reach for you, move ever closer to you, and wiggle my way into your loving heart. Teach me how to learn from you, O Perfect Trainer of Body and Soul. Amen.

May I praise you with every stretch and movement, My Perfectly-fit God.

My own wiggles and stretches to pray about…

Eating

Gone are the days when I could pop into my mouth morsels of food without giving a thought to the process.

So whatever you do, whether you eat or drink, do all for the glory of God. I Corinthians 10:31

Prayer

Thank you, My All Providing God, for the ability to still feed myself. Sometimes I become disheartened when eating turns into a difficult chore, but I ask you, My Loving God, to turn my heart to gratitude. I appreciate good appetite and all that is delicious.

Perhaps the day will come when I will need more assistance to eat than I require now, and I pray to adapt with ease to that circumstance. Let me be grateful for nourishment, O Sustaining God. Supply my soul with the love and grace to grow strong in spirit as you care for my body. Amen.

Thank you, My Sustaining God, for all that is delicious.

My own eating needs to pray about…

JOANNE ARDOLF DECKER, Ph.D.

Dressing

Until I became ill, I never noticed how much energy is required to get dressed and undressed.

> *Awake, awake, put on your strength, O Zion! Put on your beautiful garments… Isaiah 52:1a*

Prayer

O God of Enormous Energy, I plead for enough power to manage my daily dressing and undressing. Thank you for my clothing and for the caregivers who assist me. Sometimes I'd like to live in my pajamas and never face the rigors of dressing up. However, donning clothes for the day is good for both body and spirit. When I finally accomplish the task I look better, feel better, healthier and more normal.

O Fashionable God, dressing my body for the day is only one step in my daily routine. What's more, I wait for your presence to receive the blessings you have in store for me every day. Amen.

I want to dress up my body and soul for you, My Beautiful God.

My own dressing challenges to pray about…

Naps

When my eyes slim to narrow slits, my arms hang limp, and my head nods like a wafting leaf in the wind, I know the pillow calls, and I must take a nap.

Be still and know that I am God. Psalm 46:10

Prayer

My Loving God of Recuperation, you asked us to be still and know that you are God, but must I take so many naps? Let my quiet times bring recovery and greater awareness of you. I come closer and know you better in the stillness of my naps.

O Rest-filled God, when I lie down to take a nap, my thoughts are seldom with you, but rather on my weary body. When I place my head on the pillow I want my thoughts to be on you. As I nod off I want you to be the last thing on my mind and then the first when I awaken. May every breath during each nap be a prayer of praise to you, My Power and My Strength. Amen.

O God of Good Rest, I place myself in your loving arms now and always.

My own naps to pray about…

Bathroom Calls

It seems that as soon as illness strikes the body, every process becomes more complicated.

For human ways are under the eyes of the Lord… Proverbs 5:21a

Prayer

O God of All Functions, I am grateful for the marvelous operations of my body. However, most of my bodily functions have become more difficult, making mundane, personal tasks difficult in the midst of my illness.

You made all of us the same, and shared our humanity with us. You must have your reasons and explanations. I pray for patience with my body, endurance for expected and unexpected agendas, and acceptance of what is. I need your energy, resilience and might. O Most Powerful God, let me be grateful for the workings of my body. Please keep it working well. Amen.

In body and soul, I want to praise and glorify you, My Praiseworthy God.

My own bathroom calls to pray about…

Showering

A shower feels fantastic, but sometimes the effort seems greater than the reward.

Create in me a clean heart, O God, and put a new and right spirit within me. Psalm 51:10

Prayer

O Cleansing Creator, my daily shower requires great energy these days, but I am grateful for the opportunity to be cleansed in such a pleasant manner. Thank you for every warm, welcoming drop that delights my body while swishing away grunge and grime. I ask for strength and power for each shower so I can continue to be clean and energized.

My Rejuvenating Redeemer, by your death and resurrection you swished away my sins and made me whole. Your love is overwhelming, purifying, welcoming. Please grant me your cleansing ways as you purify my spirit to be more like you. Amen.

Shower me with your love, My God.

My own cleansing to pray about…

Combing My Hair

Vanity dies hard! My pride is damaged when my hair is not the way I want it.

But not a hair of your head will perish. By your endurance you will gain your souls. Luke 21: 18-19

Prayer

O Most Gorgeous God, my hair is problematic these days, and I need your help to calm my vanity. Instill in me a peace of mind that accepts who I am and how I look no matter what. Head me in the direction of true beauty.

My body is not who I am; my hair is not my identity. My soul is my essence. I want a beautiful soul, a splendid spirit, and a heart with nothing out of place. I believe that you keep track of every hair on my head, O Dearest Designer, but you didn't say that every hair must be obvious or in place! Amen.

Beautify my soul, My Beautiful God.

My own hair concerns to pray about…

Going Out

Every outing requires considerable reflection, planning and strategizing.

> *The Lord will keep your going out and your coming in from this time and forevermore. Psalm 121:8*

Prayer

O Gentle Guide, I need your assistance more than ever because my outings are complicated by inconvenience. Please steer me in the right directions, keep me safe, and grant me delight. I seek amusement in the outside world.

Be at my side, O Caring Companion, so my outings will be safe, joyful, trouble-free, and accommodating for me and for those who go with me. I pray for ease and simplicity along the way. Bring us home safely every time. Amen.

I want to safely make my way ever closer to you, My God, My Destination.

My own outings to pray about…

Preparing for Bed

The process of getting ready for bed seems endless.

> *I think of you on my bed and meditate on you in the watches of the night. Psalm 63:6*

Prayer

O Restful God, bless me with endurance, patience and stamina when bedtime comes. I need your perseverance to cope with the string of tasks that must be accomplished before I can rest every night. I am grateful for a comfortable bed, a mind and body that thrive on rest, and for a warm, peaceful place to sleep.

You are the source of harmony, serenity and rest, O Prince of Peace. Draw me close to you under the feathers of your tender, protective love. I anticipate resting in total peace with you throughout my days and nights and into eternity. Amen.

Prepare me for perfect rest with you, O Prince of Peace.

My own bedtime preparations to pray about…

Breathing

I don't take breathing for granted anymore.

Surely everyone stands as a mere breath. Psalm 39: 5:c

Prayer

My Life-giving God, my every breath depends on you. Until recently I didn't pay attention to my breathing. Now I come to you with gratitude for each breath of my life. Let me breathe in a steady, deep, and easy manner. I am thankful for the machine that assists me, but I would prefer breathing on my own.

Give me deep breaths, O Spirit of Deep Love, that fill my lungs to capacity with fresh air to nourish cells, nerves and muscles. With each breath restore my body, rejuvenate my systems, and heal me through and through. Whether I am awake or asleep I want to praise you with every breath, and be aware that my life comes from you, one breath at a time. Amen.

Breathe in me and live in me, O Spirit of Life.

My own breathing to pray about…

Sleeping

The silence, tranquility and serenity of sleep bring me comfort, consolation and rejuvenation.

In quietness and in trust shall be your strength. Isaiah 30:15b

Prayer

My Renewing God, I welcome sound sleep that revives my body and mind. You created us with a need for both effort and relaxation. Teach me to balance the two and surrender to life-giving sleep when I need it.

Each time I lay my head on the pillow, O Source of Life, take me into your loving arms to be re-created by your tender care. In faith I close my eyes trusting you will awaken me to another day or to my first glimpse of eternity. My life is in your hands. Amen.

Whether awake or asleep may my every breath praise you, O Praiseworthy God.

My own sound sleep to pray about…

Not Sleeping

Not sleeping is one of my least favorite things.

Come to me all you that are weary and are carrying heavy burdens, and I will give you rest. Matthew 11:28

Prayer

O God of My Rest, when I can't sleep, my mind dreams up illusions and delusions. Please take my restlessness and replace it with quiet peace, joyful dreams, and nearness to you. Prompt me to speak to you, turn my concerns over to you, and trust in your love.

My Omnipresent God, I know you are with me during sleepless times; that's when I want to be aware of your presence. Quiet my fears and convert my mental horrors into tranquil scenes. Teach me to pray my way through those nights. Amen.

Keep me from sleepless nights, My God of Perfect Rest.

My own sleeplessness to pray about…

Waking Up

I say to my body every day, "Up, up; time to get up!" Nonetheless, I hang in bed for a while.

O Lord, in the morning you hear my voice; in the morning I plead my case to you and watch. Psalm 5:3

Prayer

O God of All My Days, too bad I am slow to start each day. Nevertheless, I appreciate every day you grant me. You give me more days than I deserve or expect. My goal is to praise and glorify you and let you hear my voice every morning.

When I arise, My Risen God, open my eyes to your presence and nudge me to your shining light. Even before my cup of coffee, I anticipate your work in my day and await the surprises you have in store for me. Amen.

I want to awaken with you on my mind, My Loving God.

My own daily rising to pray about…

Just Sitting

When I can't budge one more minute, it seems I just want to sit.

You know when I sit down and when I rise up… Psalm 139:2a

Prayer

O God of Strength, my need to just sit and be, takes me ever closer to my weakness. During the times when my body calls for just sitting, I realize my fragility, vulnerability and the reality of my humanity. Alone, I am powerless and insufficient. Only in you, My Constant Companion, do I have strength, power and sufficiency.

When I sit to rest, I imagine myself climbing onto your knee, O Divine Love, like a child perched on her grandma's lap. I believe you will hold me secure and replenish my energy, wit, and life. Amen.

I long to sit on your knee and simply be, My Loving God.

My own sitting needs to pray about…

Receiving Care

Receiving care is like getting breakfast in bed when I have a cold. It is a good thing; too bad the cold comes with the deal.

Cast your burden on the Lord, and he will sustain you. Psalm 55:22a

Prayer

O Most Considerate God, thank you for sending good people to help and care for me. I am grateful for them in spite of wishing I didn't need them. I would rather do my daily activities myself, but you are asking me to rely on others for my humdrum routine.

You are the source of all care, My Kindhearted God. Make me an instrument of your love for my care providers. Give me a gracious attitude that fosters joy in the tasks we share. Amen.

Thank you for all who care for me, My Ever-caring God.

My own care providers to pray about…

My Faith

What would life be without my faith?

Blessed are those who have not seen and yet have believed.
John 20:29b

Prayer

O Most Loyal God, I can't imagine life without my faith. Because I believe in you, I feel loved and cared for every day. In you I find reason to get up each morning and make it through the day. Steeped in you, I can rejoice with others. I appreciate the faith community that anchors me in you.

O Everlasting God, my confidence in you gives me purpose and direction. I live not only for today but for my eternal life, my wholeness in you. My faith makes each day easier; it gives me hope for what is yet to come. Please nurture my faith by the day and root me firmly in your grace. Amen.

Fill me with faith in you, most perfect God.

My own faith to pray about…

Values Clarification

There's nothing like an illness to set priorities straight!

I will sing praises to my God all my life long. Psalm 146:2b

Prayer

O Valuable God, you know the number of my days on earth, but now I recognize there will never be enough. I don't want to squander a day or lose a moment. I crave daily choices that reflect my values. Of course you are the peak of my priorities, Dear God; family and friends are right up there near you. I pray to spend my days in wise harmony with you.

Thank you for the days you have already given me and for those that are still ahead. Walk with me and keep me on track to reach my clear, eternal day with you, My True Value. Amen.

Help me live according to my values, O Perfect God.

My own values to pray about…

Chapter IV

Blessings

Though shadows fall, the heart finds joy.

Visits

The best visits are free from anxiety and tension.

> *Contribute to the needs of the saints;
> extend hospitality to strangers. Romans 12:13*

Prayer

O My Reassuring, Welcoming God, I ask for hospitality when I have visitors. Give me energy so I can relish each visit with an open heart that cherishes each person. Demonstrate your welcoming ways through me. Let me find you in each guest, O God of Warmth. Teach me to attend to my visitors, focusing on them rather than myself. Amen.

Thank you for visitors, Dear God, and bless each one who comes my way.

My own visitors to pray about…

Cards and Calls

People take time to extend their love; what a splendid difference that makes.

…for the rendering of this ministry…overflows with many thanksgivings to God. 2 Corinthians 9:12

Prayer

O Generous God, I feel love through cards and calls sent by caring people who support us. They may not realize the spark they add to my life, but you certainly know. Please reward them and prompt me to let them know what their kindness means to me.

Like cards and calls, your love appears in surprising ways, O Delighting God. I want to be aware of your presence, your connections and your contacts. O Compassionate Communicator, teach me to read your messages of hope, love and support. Amen.

Thank you for sending encouragement from good people, and open my heart to hear your calls, My Loving God.

My own cards and calls to pray about...

Family

Like a bag of mixed nuts my family is a blend of sweetness, individuality and delight; I love them all.

The blessing of the Lord be upon you! We bless you in the name of the Lord. Psalm 128:8

Prayer

O God of All Ancestors, thank you for the amusing people I claim as family. Teach me to treasure each individual as a gift. Keep them safe on their journey toward you, and lead them to values that draw them to you and to each other.

O Loving Creator, let me never expect love from family, but be grateful for the love they give me. Let me not insist that they serve me, but be amazed for their kindness, care and generous help. Amen.

Please care for my family individually and collectively, O Caring Creator.

My own family to pray about...

Celebrations

Celebrations mark significant moments in time.

...These are the appointed festivals of the Lord... Leviticus 23:2a

Prayer

O Celebrating God, be with me as I share holidays with family and friends. When you were on earth you celebrated with your family and friends too; you understand the importance of rejoicing together to commemorate special events.

Nurture my spirit with each holiday, My Merry Maker. Help me see your loving hand in history. Let each holiday take me closer to celebrating a timeless festival with you. Amen.

I seek everlasting celebration with you, My Festive God.

My own celebrations to pray about...

Children

When the godchildren stay with us, my health and wellness improve and my spirits soar. My goddaughter once told me "When Mom and Dad come back, you turn into adults again." I guess that says it all!

...unless you change and become like children, you will never enter the kingdom of heaven. Matthew 18:3

Prayer

O God of All Ages, thank you for the children who keep me laughing.

I like to act as though I'm five, and children give me that freedom. I enjoy being imaginative, creative, witty and funny. You must be here having fun with us.

You loved children when you were on earth, Dear Jesus. They made you smile too. Bless the children of our family and keep them close to you throughout their lives. Let us enjoy unending fun and games with you. Amen.

O Loving God, bless and care for all the children of the world.

My own connections to children to pray about…

Friendship

What a blessing friends have been; now during illness they are an exceptional treasure.

…a true friend sticks closer than one's nearest kin. Proverbs 18:24b

Prayer

O Supreme Friend, you placed precious people in my life. You gave me the very best! They are friends of faith who love you and me, too. I cherish our good times and appreciate their loyalty during hard times. Please bless them and reward them for their openhanded love and service.

You are the ultimate friend, My Ceaseless Companion, the perfect model of friendship. Teach me to be a first-class friend.

Show me how to love without conditions, give without expectation, and help when needed. When I gather with friends, draw us into devoted friendship with you. Amen.

Reward my friends for all their love, My Loving God.

My own friendships to pray about…

Photos

Looking at pictures, both recent and long forgotten, is a grand way to spend a day.

He is the image of the invisible God, the firstborn of all creation. Colossians 1:15

Prayer

O God of All Memories, I marvel the photos that parade my life before my eyes. I delight in browsing and finding reminders of my life, friends left behind, and moments I still savor. My visual treasures trigger my memory and tickle my funny bone.

Thank you for being with me every moment of my life, My Picture—Perfect God.

You were there for every photo, yet you are unseen. Remain active in my life until one day you fulfill my never-ending story. Amen.

Thank you for the photos that allow me to review my life, My Memorable God.

My own everlasting story to pray about…

My Living Room Window

There are no dull moments at my living room window!

For now we see through a glass, darkly; but then face to face...
1 Corinthians 13:12

Prayer

My Transparent God, you share splendid, healing beauty with me through my living room window. Viewing the world entertains me and cheers me up. Every morning I look forward to checking out the weather: the wind or rain, clouds or sunshine. My window is my movie screen as I watch people come and go. Although I seldom get outdoors, you let me enjoy its wonders. I look forward to the views when one day I see you beyond the glass, face to face. Praise to you, Most Beautiful God. Amen.

I see your beauty everywhere, O Maker of Magnificence.

My own views of the world to pray about...

Wildlife

I envy the freedom of the animals that scurry about without obvious worries.

...I will...remember the everlasting covenant between me and
you and every living creature of all flesh that is on the earth.
Genesis 9:16

Prayer

O Beautiful Creator, how I enjoy watching the birds, squirrels, chipmunks and other animals that come into my view. They seem to live a life of serendipity, free from concerns. They fly and scamper as they please, unaware of their own beauty. They put a smile on my face.

Dear God of True Freedom, I wish I could be as carefree and spontaneous as the animals you create. They are not self absorbed. They show no signs of worry; I want that. Please create a free spirit in me that runs with freedom and flies to great heights. Yes, teach me through each animal I see. Amen.

I come running to you, My Perfect Creator.

My own views of animals to pray about…

Movies

I enjoy putting on a video and curling up under my blanket to be taken to distant lands, imaginative realms, and into fascinating plots and life situations.

My help comes from the Lord, who made heaven and earth.
Psalm 120:2

Prayer

O Entertaining God, you know that I love movies, and I want to continue making good choices among them. Let their plots and pictures bring me closer to you; never put distance between us.

Distract me from pain and stress as I imagine myself alongside the characters and action.

I pray for the entertainers, that they have opportunities to share their talents and grow closer to you. Show them, O Master Maker, how to make movies that are uplifting and fun for the ride. I am not the only one who needs movies that are good for health, moods, and attitudes. Amen.

Be the star of my life, Dear God of True Entertainment.

My own movie imagination to pray about...

Television

To be able to sit in comfort and let the world come to me, is a wonder indeed.

...for what can be seen is temporary, but what cannot be seen is eternal. II Corinthians, 4:18b

Prayer

O Unseen God, thank you for inspiring the invention of television. It brings me an array of amazing people and places around the world. We are able to tune in to each other's lives and keep track of world events through television.

Show us, O Caring Commentator, how to use this great invention for ongoing good. Teach us to use information at our fingertips to promote peace, good will, generosity, kindness and love around the world. Amen.

Teach me to use information to stay close to you, O Compassionate Correspondent.

My own television viewing to pray about...

Reading

Nothing measures up to the satisfaction of holding a book in my hands, reading the printed words, and feeling the pages as I turn them one by one.

Your word is a lamp to my feet and a light to my path. Psalm 119:105

Prayer

O Author of Life, much of my life learning began with reading. Now, I want to be attentive to the written words in scripture, books, newspapers and magazines. Wonderful information surrounds me, but it is lost if my mind doesn't cooperate and my body wants to sleep. When I read, keep me alert to comprehend and enjoy the information before me. Let me nap at other times, not when I want to read please! Amen.

Let my reading bring glory to you and enjoyment to me, O Glorious God.

My own reading time to pray about...

Love

Love makes the world go 'round!

> *Love is patient; love is kind; love is not envious or boastful or arrogant or rude. 1 Corinthians 13:4*

Prayer

O Most Affectionate God, thank you for the loving relationships and tender moments I've shared in my life. I have had a glimpse of your love and gentleness. You are always close, My Loving God, but I cannot feel your company without touch. I appreciate the human closeness that leads me to comprehend you.

Teach me to express my love, care and affection for the loved ones you place in my life. They all reflect your goodness, warmth and gentleness, My Sensitive God. Let me be an instrument of your love. Amen.

> *Teach me how to love, O Perfect Lover.*

My own love filled relationships to pray about…

My Special Person

In my youth I thought intimacy was always surrounded by romance; I know better now.

> *…for your love is better than wine. Song of Solomon 1:2*

Prayer

O Most Special God, you gifted me with a special person whose kindness is a profound treasure. I thank you for this loving relationship and for the tender moments we share. This love shows me the power of love; you show me a glimpse of your love and gentleness.

We find intimacy in ordinary moments of kindness and caring. Even the preparation and serving of my breakfast show thoughtfulness that touches my soul. Helping me dress or bringing a blanket says, "I love you" as certainly as the words. My Affectionate God, teach me to express my love, care and affection for you through my special person. Let me be an instrument of your love. Amen.

Teach me how to love, O Perfect Lover.

My own special person to pray about…

Hugs

It took me a long time to learn how to hug, and now I don't ever want to lose that touch.

…steadfast love surrounds those who trust in the Lord.
Psalm 32:10b

Prayer

You are the source of all affection, My Loving God, and I appreciate the stockpile of hugs gathered over my lifetime. You furnish me with loving people who demonstrate their love through hugs, and I am grateful. When you were on earth you expressed your love through compassionate words and deeds. I would have enjoyed being with you.

Please keep me well enough to give and receive affection, My Expressive God. I want to feel your love through others and enjoy the attention of family and friends. Amen.

Hug me tight in body and soul, My Loving God.

My own hugs to pray about…

Music

To tap into music is to brush the lives of people and hear their sounds singing from their hearts.

I will sing and make melody to the Lord. Psalm 27:6b

Prayer

O Caring Conductor, I welcome the phenomenal sounds of music that bring melodies to my ears. From angels singing at your birth to today's popular songs, music is a key to human expression. I love to sing, tap my toes and hear healing harmonies.

Grant me appreciation of your music in my life, O Master Music Maker. Teach me to live in tempo with you, sing according to your compositions, and harmonize with others to praise you. I want to be a laudable performer in your symphony of life. Amen.

Thank you for the healing nature of music, O Master Musician.

My own melodies to pray about…

Traveling

The memories are still vivid of God's beauty everywhere I traveled over the years.

I believe I shall see the goodness of the Lord in the land of the living. Psalm 27:13

Prayer

O Maker of Magnificence, I close my eyes and still relish your sunsets, billowy clouds on mountain peaks, ocean waves splashing shimmering rocks, and wild berries calling to be picked. Although I cannot wander as I once did, my mind is filled with travel logs for reminiscing.

Thank you for your beauty everywhere, O Dazzling Deity. This world is filled with your wonders, and I still have heaven to look forward to. Prepare me for my adventure into paradise with colors, spectacles and scenes that are beyond my current senses. I believe your eternal wonders will be first class, and I don't want to miss them. Amen.

Heal me with life's beauty, My God of Glory.

My own travel memories to pray about…

Being Home

I am grateful for this safe and cozy place, whether I feel good or bad.

> ...the Lord has comforted his people, and will have compassion on his suffering ones. Isaiah 50:1

Prayer

You bless me with a comfy place to dwell, Dear Indwelling God. My home offers comfort to me, my family and visitors. It is not large or elaborate, but it keeps us safe, warm, dry and at peace. Thank you for this special place. Permeate this home with your presence.

O God of Contentment, my home contains my favorite things that keep me engaged in life. I appreciate my many interests. There are no dull moments when I serve you and others from right here at home. Amen.

I know you are with me, My Living God, whether I am at home or away.

My own home to pray about…

My Computer

Although I couldn't tell you how it works, my computer is the social center of my life.

> *Wisdom is at home in the mind of one who has understanding.* Proverbs 14:33

Prayer

The computer is an amazing advancement in my lifetime, Dear Innovative God. I am able to access information, link to other people, and be in touch with the world. Information is at my fingertips; an astounding gift to appreciate.

My Enlightening God, enlighten everyone to be resourceful for the good of the world and each other. Let me use my computer for fun and communication, but bring glory to you. Amen.

Thank you for the joys I find in my computer, My Perfect Communicator.

My own computer experiences to pray about…

Flowers

Flowers have enchanted me throughout my lifetime, but now I relish them more than ever.

>*…consider the lilies of the field, how they grow; they neither toil nor spin… Matthew 6:28b*

Prayer

O Beautiful God, flower colors, shapes, textures, petals, leaves and fragrances make me smile and heal my body and soul. Thank you for your artistic floral creations.

Teach me, O Adorable One, to be more flower-like in my life. I want to bloom where I'm planted, lean toward your light, be patient with my growth, slow and gentle to show my colors, and accept my humble place within your garden. Nurture me, O Gentle Gardener, to become the person you want me to be now and always. Amen.

Your flowers bring healing to my soul, My Beautiful God.

My own flowers to pray about…

Sunsets

Every sunset represents both an ending and a new beginning.

…his glory is above earth and heaven. Psalm 148:13b

Prayer

O Sun-filled Divinity, your sunsets captivate me whenever I see them. They are one of my favorite things. They enhance my health and healing. I have tried to capture many of them on film, but I never succeeded. Your art is too brilliant, O Most Creative Artist.

Your colors, clouds, streaks and stripes form surprising combinations. Such art work is only a shadow of your glory. I yearn to see your face surrounded by new colors I have not yet witnessed, O Beautiful God. That sunset will be the ultimate ending and beginning in my life. Amen.

Praise the Lord, all ye sunrises and sunsets!

My own sunsets to pray about…

Night Skies

God's glory shines, even at night.

> *He brought him outside and said, "Look toward heaven and count the stars, if you are able to count them"...*
> *Genesis 15:5a*

Prayer

O Wondrous God, how I enjoy the night skies filled with stars, the moon, planets and moonlit clouds! Each star seems to be a peep hole into heaven. All your heavenly bodies make me feel tiny in your cosmic universe. Looking up gives me true perspective of your greatness and my true size. How can one see your glory in the night and not believe in you?

Oh God of All Splendor, your beauty fills me with awe. Thank you for my vision that allows me to be enchanted by your magical majesty. A nighttime view lifts my head towards you where I feel wrapped in your glory. Shine your light on me. Amen.

I want to be a star in the heavens with you, Most Beautiful God.

My own views of night skies to pray about...

Humor

What a gift God gave us when he fashioned us with silliness in our very core!

> *A cheerful heart is a good medicine... Proverbs 17:22a*

Prayer

My Humorous God, you must giggle with us every day when you watch us here on earth. I'm sure you enjoy a hearty laugh when we do absurd things. Thank you for giving us the capacity to laugh in daily life.

Sometimes finding humor in the midst of illness is not easy. My God of Good Wit, help me uncover amusement in gloomy corners and find chuckles in dismal moments. I fancy the bright side of life where you are, O Perfect Light. Amen.

Thank you for humor, fun and laughter, O Fun-loving God.

My own sense of humor to pray about…

Gratitude

With gratitude as a foundation I believe I have a better chance to live a healing life.

Give thanks in all circumstances, for this is the will of God in Christ Jesus for you. I Thessalonians 5:18

Prayer

O Gracious God, grant me a satisfied heart regardless of what comes my way. I want to be ready to receive your healing. I believe an attitude of gratitude places me close to you. Teach me to recount the miracles you grant me and tell others how appreciative I am.

My Bountiful God, teach me to focus on health not illness, on what I have, not what I wish for. Help me emphasize positives rather than negatives, and direct my attention to gains, not losses. Amen.

In all things I want to be grateful to you, O Generous God.

My own gratitude to pray about…

Going Home

Home is where my heart is.

> *"Those who love me will keep my word, and my Father will love them, and we will come to them and make our home with them. John 14:23*

Prayer

O Never-ending God, since learning of my illness, I ponder my eternal home with you more than ever. Even though I don't dwell on my death, my mortality is absolute. I await going home to you.
O Divine Trust, I anticipate the fulfillment of your promises. I pray to be worthy and ready to say "yes" to you. Welcome me into your loving arms where I can be at home with you. Home is where the heart is. I place my heart in your heart, My God of Golden Promises. Amen.

Let me be forever at home with you, My Everlasting God.

My own destination to pray about…

O Maker of Magnificence,
I find your beauty everywhere.
You fill my life with love and gifts,
and now I long to see your face.
Joanne Ardolf Decker